CW01506560

by Iain Gray

PUBLISHING

WRITING *to* REMEMBER

LangSyne
PUBLISHING
WRITING *to* REMEMBER

79 Main Street, Newtongrange,
Midlothian EH22 4NA
Tel: 0131 344 0414   Fax: 0845 075 6085
E-mail: info@lang-syne.co.uk
www.langsyneshop.co.uk

Design by Dorothy Meikle
Printed by Printwell Ltd
© Lang Syne Publishers Ltd 2017

ISBN 978-1-85217-669-3

Pugh

MOTTO:
Such is the way to immortality.

CREST:
A dolphin.

NAME variations include:
Pew
Pughe

Chapter one:

Origins of Welsh surnames

by Iain Gray

If you don't know where you came from, you won't know where you're going is a frequently quoted observation and one that has a particular resonance today when there has been a marked upsurge in interest in genealogy, with increasing numbers of people curious to trace their family roots.

Main sources for genealogical research include census returns and official records of births, marriages and deaths – and the key to unlocking the detail they contain is obviously a family surname, one that has been 'inherited' and passed from generation to generation.

No matter our station in life, we all have a surname – but it was not until about the middle of the fourteenth century that the practice of being identified by a particular, or 'fixed', surname became commonly established throughout the British Isles.

Previous to this, it was normal for a person to be identified through the use of only a forename.

Wales, however, known in the Welsh language as *Cymru*, is uniquely different – with the use of what are known as patronymic names continuing well into the fifteenth century and, in remote rural areas, up until the early nineteenth century.

Patronymic names are ones where a son takes his father's forename, or Christian name, as his surname.

Examples of patronymic names throughout the British Isles include 'Johnson', indicating 'son of John', while specifically in Scotland 'son of' was denoted by the prefix Mc or Mac – with 'MacDonald', for example, meaning 'son of Donald.'

Early Welsh law, known as *Cyfraith Hywel*, *The Law of Hywel*, introduced by Hywel the Good, who ruled from Prestatyn to Pembroke between 915 AD and 950 AD, stipulated that a person's name should indicate their ancestry – the name in effect being a type of 'family tree.'

This required the prefixes *ap* or *ab* – derived from *mab*, meaning 'son of' being placed before the person's baptismal name.

In the case of females, the suffixes *verch* or *ferch*, sometimes shortened to *vch* or *vz* would be attached to their Christian name to indicate 'daughter of.'

In some cases, rather than being known for

example as *Llewellyn ap Thomas – Llewellyn son of Thomas –* Llewellyn's name would incorporate an 'ancestral tree' going back much earlier than his father.

One source gives the example of *Llewellyn ap Thomas ap Dafydd ap Evan ap Owen ap John –* meaning *Llewellyn son of Thomas son of Dafydd son of Evan son of Owen son of John.*

This leads to great confusion, to say the least, when trying to trace a person's ancestry back to a particular family – with many people having the forenames, for example, of Llewellyn, Thomas, Owen or John.

The first Act of Union between Wales and England that took place in 1536 during the reign of Henry VIII required that all Welsh names be registered in an Anglicised form – with *Hywel*, for example, becoming Howell, or Powell, and *Gruffydd* becoming Griffiths.

An early historical example of this concerns William ap John Thomas, standard bearer to Henry VIII, who became William Jones.

In many cases – as in Davies and Williams – an s was simply added to the original patronymic name, while in other cases the prefix *ap* or *ab* was contracted to *p* or *b* to prefix the name – as in *ab Evan* to form Bevan and *ap Richard* to form Pritchard.

Other original Welsh surnames – such as Morgan, originally *Morcant* – derive from ancient Celtic sources, while others stem from a person's physical characteristics – as in *Gwyn* or *Wynne* a nickname for someone with fair hair, *Gough* or *Gooch* denoting someone with red hair or a ruddy complexion, *Gethin* indicating swarthy or ugly and *Lloyd* someone with brown or grey hair.

With many popular surnames found today in Wales being based on popular Christian names such as John, this means that what is known as the 'stock' or 'pool' of names is comparatively small compared to that of common surnames found in England, Scotland and Ireland.

This explains why, in a typical Welsh village or town with many bearers of a particular name not necessarily being related, they were differentiated by being known, for example, as 'Jones the butcher', 'Jones the teacher' and 'Jones the grocer.'

Another common practice, dating from about the nineteenth century, was to differentiate among families of the same name by prefixing it with the mother's surname or hyphenating the name.

The history of the origins and development of Welsh surnames is inextricably bound up with the nation's frequently turbulent history and its rich culture.

Speaking a Celtic language known as Brythonic, which would gradually evolve into Welsh, the natives were subjected to Roman invasion in 48 AD, and in the following centuries to invasion by the Anglo-Saxons, Vikings and Normans.

Under England's ruthless and ambitious Edward I, the nation was fortified with castles between 1276 and 1295 to keep the 'rebellious' natives in check – but this did not prevent a series of bloody uprisings against English rule that included, most notably, Owain Glyndŵr's rebellion in 1400.

Politically united with England through the first Act of Union in 1536, becoming part of the Kingdom of Great Britain in 1707 and part of the United Kingdom in 1801, it was in 1999 that *Cynulliad Cenedlaethol Cymru*, the National Assembly for Wales, was officially opened by the Queen.

Welsh language and literature has flourished throughout the nation's long history.

In what is known as the Heroic Age, early Welsh poets include the late sixth century Taliesin and Aneirin, author of *Y Gododdin*.

Discovered in a thirteenth century manuscript but thought to date from anywhere between the seventh and eleventh centuries, it refers to the kingdom of Gododdin that took in south-east Scotland and

Northumberland and was part of what was once the Welsh territory known as *Hen Ogledd*, *The Old North*.

Commemorating Gododdin warriors who were killed in battle against the Angles of Bernicia and Deira at Catraith in about 600 AD, the manuscript – known as *Llyfr Aneirin*, *Book of Aneirin* – is now in the precious care of Cardiff City Library.

Other important early works by Welsh poets include the fourteenth century *Red Book of Hergest*, now held in the Bodleian Library, Oxford, and the *White Book of Rhydderch*, kept in the National Library of Wales, Aberystwyth.

William Morgan's translation of the Bible into Welsh in 1588 is hailed as having played an important role in the advancement of the Welsh language, while in 1885 Dan Isaac Davies founded the first Welsh language society.

It was in 1856 that Evan James and his son James James composed the rousing Welsh national anthem *Hen Wlad Fynhadad – Land of My Fathers*, while in the twentieth century the poet Dylan Thomas gained international fame and acclaim with poems such as *Under Milk Wood*.

The nation's proud cultural heritage is also celebrated through *Eisteddfod Genedlaethol Cymru*, the National Eisteddfod of Wales, the annual festival of music, literature and performance that is held across the nation and which traces its roots back to 1176 when Rhys ap Gruffyd, who ruled the territory of Deheubarth from 1155 to 1197, hosted a magnificent festival of poetry and song at his court in Cardigan.

The 2011 census for Wales unfortunately shows that the number of people able to speak the language has declined from 20.8% of the population of just under 3.1 million in 2001 to 19% – but overall the nation's proud culture, reflected in its surnames, still flourishes.

Many Welsh families proudly boast the heraldic device known as a Coat of Arms, as featured on our front cover.

The central motif of the Coat of Arms would originally have been what was borne on the shield of a warrior to distinguish himself from others on the battlefield.

Not featured on the Coat of Arms, but highlighted on page three, is the family motto and related crest – with the latter frequently different from the central motif.

Echoes of a far distant past can still be found in our surnames and they can be borne with pride in commemoration of our forebears.

Chapter two:

On the frontline

Although a surname that, in common with many others found throughout the British Isles today derives from a popular forename introduced in the wake of the Norman Conquest of 1066, Welsh bearers of the Pugh name have roots that stretch back much earlier in time.

The forename is 'Hugh', derived from the Old French 'Hu(gh)e, an abbreviated form of a number of Germanic compound names indicating 'heart', 'mind' or 'spirit.'

As a forename, it became popular with the Normans in veneration of St Hugh of Lincoln, also known as Hugh of Burgundy and Hugh of Avalon, who established the first Carthusian monastery in England before his death in 1200.

It is from the forename 'Hugh' that the surname 'Hughes' derives, while 'Pugh' stems from the original Welsh patronymic form of 'ap Hughes', indicating 'son of Hugh.'

The 'Pew' spelling variant, meanwhile, derives from the 'Hew' form of 'Hugh.'

To unravel the complex genealogical skein of

those who came to bear the Pugh name, we have to travel back through the dim mists of time to a period that pre-dates the Norman Conquest and to what is now present-day Montgomeryshire – one of the thirteen historic Welsh counties.

It was here that the chieftain Cadwallader ap Jevaf, whom early sources refer to as 'King of Wales', ruled – and it is from him that the Pughes claim descent.

Details concerning his violent life and times are obscure, but what is known is that he succeeded his father and his uncle as 'King of Wales' in 972 AD – in all probability by killing them – but was himself slain in battle against the Anglo-Saxons in 984 AD.

The Anglo-Saxons were those Germanic tribes who invaded and settled in the south and east of the island of Britain from about the early fifth century.

Composed of the Jutes, from the area of the Jutland Peninsula in modern Denmark, the Saxons from Lower Saxony, in modern Germany and the Angles from the Angeln area of Germany – it was the latter who gave the name 'Engla land', or 'Aengla land' – better known as 'England.'

They held sway from approximately 550 to 1066, with the main kingdoms those of Sussex, Wessex, Northumbria, Mercia, Kent, East Anglia and Essex after having largely usurped the power of the indigenous

Britons, such as Cadwallader ap Jevaf – who referred to them as 'Saeson' or 'Saxones.'

It is from this that the Welsh term for 'English people' of 'Saeson' derives, the Scottish-Gaelic 'Sasannach' and the Irish-Gaelic 'Sasanach'.

Cadwallader ap Jevaf's descendants – later to be known as the Pughs – meanwhile continued to hold their ancient seat at Llanerchydol.

But a much greater threat to their independence than Anglo-Saxon swords and battle-axes came in the wake of the Norman Conquest – a pivotal event in subsequent English and Welsh history

By 1066, England had become a nation with several powerful competitors to the throne.

In what were extremely complex family, political and military machinations, the monarch was Harold II, who had succeeded to the throne following the death of Edward the Confessor.

But his right to the throne was contested by two powerful competitors – his brother-in-law King Harold Hardrada of Norway, in alliance with Tostig, Harold II's brother, and Duke William II of Normandy.

In what has become known as The Year of Three Battles, Hardrada invaded England and gained victory over the English king on September 20 at the battle of Fulford, in Yorkshire.

Five days later, however, Harold II decisively defeated his brother-in-law and brother at the battle of Stamford Bridge.

But he had little time to celebrate his victory, having to immediately march south from Yorkshire to encounter a mighty invasion force led by Duke William that had landed at Hastings, in East Sussex.

Harold's battle-hardened but exhausted force confronted the Normans on October 14, drawing up a strong defensive position at the top of Senlac Hill and building a shield wall to repel William's cavalry and infantry.

The Normans suffered heavy losses, but through a combination of the deadly skill of their archers and the ferocious determination of their cavalry they eventually won the day.

Morale had collapsed on the battlefield as word spread through the ranks that Harold, the last of the Anglo-Saxon kings, had been killed.

William was declared King of England on December 25, and the complete subjugation of his Anglo-Saxon subjects followed.

Those Normans who had fought on his behalf were rewarded with the lands of Anglo-Saxons and became known as Anglo-Normans.

Those who later subdued large parts of Wales

and protected themselves behind the forbidding walls of mighty fortresses were known as Cambro-Normans, with 'Cambro' derived from 'Cambria', the Latinised form of Cymru, or Wales.

Modern day County Montgomeryshire, original heartland of the Pughs and known as *Sir Drefaldwyn*, with 'Sir' denoting 'County' was literally on the frontline of invasion, in the same manner as the Borders region of Scotland was on the frontline of English invasion.

Also known as Maldwyn, its close proximity to the border between Wales and England – known in Welsh as *Y Mers*, in Latin as *Marchia Walliae*, and in English as *The Welsh Marches* or *The March of Wales* – made it particularly susceptible to invasion.

The modern-day town of Montgomery, for example, takes its name from Roger de Montgomerie, the principal counsellor of William the Conqueror who was created 1st Earl of Shrewsbury and who died in 1094.

In September of 1267, Montgomery was the scene of one of the key events in the frequently turbulent history of Wales.

This was through the signing of the Treaty of Montgomery, also known as the Anglo-Cambrian Treaty – its importance lying in the fact that Henry III of

England officially recognised Llywelyn ap Gruffudd, ruler of Gwynedd and a grandson of Llywelyn the Great, as Prince of Wales – a proud title better known to the Welsh as *Tywysog Cymru*.

It was the first and only time that a ruler of Gwynedd was recognised as having the right to rule over Wales – but the treaty also stipulated that Llywelyn had to pay homage to the king as his lord superior.

Henry III died in 1272 and was succeeded by the ruthlessly ambitious Edward I, who declared war on Llywelyn four years later.

Llywelyn, known to posterity as Llywelyn the Last, was tricked into a meeting at Builth Wells castle in December of 1282 with a number of 'Lords of the Marches' and killed.

His demoralised army was then destroyed and his brother Dafydd ap Gruffudd was captured in June of the following year and, taken to Shrewsbury, subjected to the horrific ordeal of being hanged, drawn and quartered.

Edward ordered the building or repair of at least 17 castles and, to put a humiliating seal on his dominance over the Welsh in 1302 proclaimed his son and heir, the future Edward II, as *Tywysog Cymru*.

Chapter three:

Royalists and radicals

Bearers of the Pugh named proved staunch Royalists during the bitter seventeenth century English Civil War.

King Charles I had incurred the wrath of Parliament by his insistence on the 'divine right' of monarchs, and added to this was Parliament's fear of Catholic 'subversion' against the state and the king's stubborn refusal to grant demands for religious and constitutional concessions.

Matters came to a head with the outbreak of the war in 1642, with Parliamentary forces, known as the New Model Army and commanded by Oliver Cromwell and Sir Thomas Fairfax, arrayed against the Royalist army of the king.

In what became an increasingly bloody and complex conflict, spreading to Wales, Scotland and Ireland and with rapidly shifting loyalties on both sides, the king was eventually captured and executed in January of 1649 on the orders of Parliament.

Rowland Pugh, a descendant of the noted Pugh family of Mathafarn, Montgomeryshire – one of whose prominent members had been the fifteenth century poet

Dafydd Llwyd ap Llywelyn – had his house burned to the ground by Parliamentary soldiers in 1644 because of his Royalist sympathies.

In common with a number of other members of the family, he had held prominent office – serving from 1609 to 1626 as Sheriff of Montgomeryshire and, in 1631, as Sheriff of Merioneth.

A member of a prominent Pugh family from the Creuddyn, in the north of Wales, Gwilym Pugh, also known as William Pugh, was not only a Catholic poet but also a Royalist officer who held the rank of captain.

One of his poems, written in 1648, stated that the evils then afflicting Britain were God's punishment for the abandonment of "the true religion."

A victim of religious persecution, Ellis Pugh subsequently gained a rather unusual claim to literary fame as the author of the first book in Welsh to be published in America.

Born in 1656 at Penrhos, near Tyddyn-y-garreg, Merionethshire, he was aged 18 when he joined the religious grouping known as The Friends of Truth, nicknamed Quakers after its founder, George Fox, told a judge to "tremble at the name of the Lord."

Rejecting a professional ministry and refusing to pay tithes or swear oaths to the Established Church, the Quakers were subjected to persecution and many found refuge in Pennsylvania, which William Penn had founded as a Quaker colony in 1682.

Many Welsh Quakers left their homeland for Pennsylvania, and among their number was Ellis Pugh, who arrived there in 1687.

Settling with his family near a township named Gwynedd, now in Montgomery County, Pennsylvania, he toiled as a farmer while also ministering to his fellow Welsh Quakers.

He died in 1718, leaving behind the manuscript of a semi-historical novel depicting the persecution and plight of Quakers back in his homeland and which he had titled *Annerch i'r Cymru – Salutation to the Welsh*.

Printed in 1721, it became the first Welsh language book to be published in the New World – while an English translation was published in 1727 as *A Salutation to the Britons*.

Interest in the book resurfaced many years later, with the English translation reprinted in London in both 1782 and 1801.

A supporter of the early nineteenth century Reform Bill, William Pugh was the colourful Welsh entrepreneur and radical landlord born in 1783 at Pennant, Berriw, Montgomeryshire.

The son of a wealthy landowner and lawyer who had also introduced banking to the town of

Newtown, Pugh studied law and was called to the bar in 1813.

But his interests lay in his native Montgomeryshire and it was here, settled in the family mansion at Brynllywarch, that he was responsible for a number of improvements that included, from 1815 to 1819, the extension of the Montgomeryshire canal to Newtown and the macadamizing of turnpike roads throughout the county

Serving as a magistrate, it was through his popularity in the county that he was instrumental in preventing serious food riots breaking out during the particularly harsh winter of 1830, while he also organised local support for the Reform Bill.

Passed in 1832 and with its supporters dubbed 'radicals', the Reform Act revolutionised the voting system – extending the franchise from the exclusive preserve of the landed classes to the middle classes.

It would not be until 1867, however, that the franchise would be further extended to skilled workers – while universal suffrage did not come into effect until the Representation of the People Acts of 1918 and 1928.

William Pugh, meanwhile, as a local representative of the Society for the Diffusion of Useful Knowledge, promoted both popular education and a newspaper, the *Montgomeryshire Herald*.

He also promoted the flannel trade in Newtown and the surrounding area – but a slump in the trade and the failure of the bank his father had set up forced him to sell up his interest in 1835 and settle in Caen, France.

It was here that Pugh, who had done so much to improve the original Pugh heartland of Montgomeryshire, died in 1842.

Another noted Montgomeryshire bearer of the Pugh name was David Pugh, the entrepreneur, landowner and Conservative Party politician born in 1789.

Having made his wealth in the tea trade, he served as High Sheriff of Montgomeryshire in 1823 and, from 1832 to 1847, as Member of Parliament (MP) for Montgomery Boroughs.

He died in 1861, having donated a site in Newtown for the building of St David's Church; his family's 2000-acre estate of Llanerchydol Hall, meanwhile, their home since 1776, was split up and sold in 1912.

In contemporary Welsh politics, Alun Pugh is the Labour Party politician and former National Assembly for Wales Government Minister for Culture, Welsh Language and Sport born in 1955 in Llwynypia, Mid Glamorgan.

Elected to the Assembly in 1999 to represent the Clwyd West seat, other government posts he has held include Deputy Minister for Economic Development.

Defeated at the 2007 election to the Assembly, he was also defeated three years later when standing for the Arfon constituency; in 2007, meanwhile, he was appointed director of the environmental charity the Snowdonia Society.

One particularly selfless bearer of the Pugh name was Herbert Pugh, the only clergyman to date to have been awarded the George Cross – the highest gallantry award for civilians.

Born in Johannesburg in 1898, he served on the Western Front during the First World War as a medical orderly with the South African Field Ambulance and, settling in England after the conflict, became a Congregational Church minister.

Serving as a minister at Camberley Congregational Church from 1924 to 1927 and then at Christ Church, Frien Barnet, Middlesex, on the outbreak of the Second World War in 1939 he became an RAF chaplain, serving at RAF Bridgnorth, Shropshire.

Posted in 1941 to Takoradi, on the Gold Coast, he embarked on the troop ship SS *Anselm* that was carrying 1,200 British Army Royal Marine and RAF personnel en route to serve in the North African campaign.

Tragedy struck about 300 miles north of the Azores on July 5 when *Anselm* was torpedoed by the German submarine *U-96*.

Chaos ensued as the resulting explosion caused extensive damage below decks, leaving many men trapped in some of the converted holds.

While many officers, according to one survivor, left the stricken vessel in boats without attempting to help their men, Pugh remained aboard to help launch lifeboats and liferafts and tend to the wounded.

As *Anselm's* bow sank deeper into the sea, Herbert Pugh pleaded with some Royal Marines to lower him by rope to the wrecked hold that held trapped RAF personnel.

Trying to persuade him that this would be suicidal, Pugh persisted, telling them: "Where my men are, I have to be" and: "My love of God is greater than my fear of death."

The marines reluctantly agreed to his request and accordingly lowered him into the hold – and the last they saw of him was praying with the doomed men as the water reached his shoulders.

Anselm sank shortly afterwards with a loss of more than 300 lives – including that of Herbert Pugh.

It was not until after the war that stories from survivors about his bravery and selflessness began to appear in British newspapers and, in 1947, he was duly honoured when George VI presented his widow with the George Cross her husband had so rightly earned.

Chapter four:

On the world stage

Born in Memphis in 1959, Willard Pugh is the American actor whose many film credits include the 1982 *The Color Purple*, the 1997 *Air Force One* and, from 1990, *RoboCop 2*, while Zachary Levi Pugh is the actor and director better known by his stage name of Zachary Levi.

Born of Welsh ancestry in 1980 in Lake Charles, Indiana, he first took to the stage when aged six, playing in productions that include *Grease* and *The Wizard of Oz*.

Best known for his role of Chuck Bartowski in the television series *Chuck*, he has also starred in the sitcom *Less than Perfect* and the 2013 *Thor: The Dark World*.

Back in the early Pugh homeland of Wales, **Robert Pugh** is the actor born in 1950 in The Tynte, Mountain Ash.

His many television credits include the roles of former British Prime Minister Harold Wilson in the 2005 Channel 4 drama *Longford* and as Herman Göring in the 2006 BBC drama *Nuremberg: Nazis on Trial*.

Other credits include the 2007 ITV 1 drama

The Time of Your Life, *Doctor Who* and the role of Welsh leader Owain Glyndŵr in the 2012 BBC adaptation of Shakespeare's *Henry IV, Part I*.

A co-creator and co-writer, along with Bob Carroll, Jr., of the American television comedy series *I Love Lucy*, **Madelyn Pugh** was born in 1921 in Indiana.

Graduating in 1942 from the Indiana University School of Journalism, it was after moving to California that she met Carroll while working as a radio writer for CBS.

Forging a writing partnership with Carroll that lasted for more than 50 years, they penned scripts for Lucille Ball's radio show *My Favourite Husband*.

This led to television's *I Love Lucy*, with Ball starring beside her real life husband Desi Arnaz.

The series ran throughout the 1950s and Pugh and Carroll were nominated for three Emmy Awards for their work, while they also wrote episodes for the television 'spin-offs' *The Lucy Show*, *Here's Lucy*, *The Lucy-Desi Comedy Hour* and, from 1986, *Life with Lucy*.

Also sometimes credited as Madelyn Pugh Davis, Madelyn Davis or Madelyn Martin, she died in 2011.

A leading West End and Broadway theatre producer, along with his business partner Dafydd Rogers, **David Pugh** was born in London in 1959.

Their first production, *Art*, at the Wyndhams Theatre in the West End, starring Tom Courtenay, Ken Stott and Albert Finney, ran for eight years and was the winner of both the Olivier Award and the *Evening Standard* Theatre Award.

Starring Alan Alda, Alfred Molina and Victor Garber, the production also ran on Broadway and won a Tony Award for Best Play.

Other major award-winning productions include the 'jukebox musical' *The Blues Brothers*, which toured throughout the world for fifteen years, *God of Carnage*, *Heroes* and Noel Coward's *Brief Encounter*.

Their stage production of *Calendar Girls*, which opened in the West End in 2009, is rated at the time of writing as the most successful UK touring play of all time, while their production of the play adaptation of the film *The Full Monty* opened in 2013 at the Lyceum Theatre Sheffield before embarking on a tour throughout the rest of the UK and Ireland.

In the equally creative world of fashion, **Gareth Pugh**, born in Sunderland in 1981, is the English designer whose creations have been worn by stars who include Kylie Minogue, Beyoncé and Lady Gaga.

Bearers of the Pugh name have also excelled in the highly creative world of sport.

In the rough and tumble that is the game of

rugby union, **Richie Pugh** is the Wales international player who made his debut for his country in 2005 in a tour match against the USA.

Born in Swansea in 1983, the open-side flanker was part of the team that won the Melrose Cup at the 2009 Rugby World Cup Sevens, while clubs he has played for include the Ospreys, Exeter Chiefs and the Scarlets.

On the tennis court, **Jim Pugh** is the American former doubles specialist who in 1989 was ranked No. 1 in the World Doubles ranking.

Born in 1964 in Burbank, California and the winner of three Grand Slam men's doubles titles – one Wimbledon and two Australian opens – he is an inductee of the Intercollegiate Tennis Association (ITA) Hall of Fame.

From sport to the world of art, **Clifton Ernest Pugh** was the Australian artist particularly noted for his portraits and landscapes.

Born in 1924 in Richmond, Victoria, he attended evening classes to study cartoon drawing before taking classes in life drawing at the South Australian School of Arts and Crafts, Adelaide.

Serving in New Guinea with the Australian forces during the Second World War, following the end of the conflict he studied at the National Gallery of

Victoria Art School before, in 1951, buying 15 acres of bushland northeast of Melbourne.

Naming it *Dunmoochin*, it became a 'commune' for fellow artists and potters and, in 1957, Pugh held his first solo show at the Victoria Artists Society Gallery, Melbourne.

Further exhibitions followed across the world as his fame grew – with works that include *Portrait of a Woman* – his wife Marlene Pugh – and a 1972 portrait of Australian Prime Minister Gough Whitlam.

The winner on three occasions of Australia's prestigious Archibald Prize for art, he was made an Officer of the Order of Australia in 1985 while, shortly before his death in 1990, he was appointed the Australian War Memorials' official artist to mark the 75th anniversary of the First World War Gallipoli landings.

In a different artistic genre, **Jonathan Pugh** is the English cartoonist who has worked for publications that range from *The Times*, *The Independent* and *Daily Mail* newspapers to magazines that include *Private Eye* and *Country Life*.

Born in Worcester in 1962, he has also worked on book illustrations and for the world of advertising.

On a musical note, **James Pugh** is the American trombonist and composer who has worked with solo artists and bands that include Chick Corea, Steely Dan, Paul Simon, Michael Jackson, Frank Sinatra, Pink Floyd and Madonna.

Born in 1950 in Camden, New Jersey, he is a recipient of a National Academy of Recording Arts and Sciences' Virtuoso Award for tenor trombone.

In the genre of 'pop punk', **Will Pugh**, born in 1984 in Conyers, Georgia, is the vocalist for the American band Cartel – whose internationally best-selling albums include the 2005 *Chroma* and, from 2012, *Collider*.

From music to the written word, **Sheenagh Pugh** is the award-winning British poet, novelist and translator born in Birmingham in 1950.

After studying languages at Bristol University, she lived for a time in Wales – where her collection of poetry *Stonelight* won the 2000 Wales Book of the Year Award.

Now resident in Shetland, she was also a winner on two occasions of the Cardiff International Poetry Competition, while her 2002 poetry collection *The Beautiful Lie* was shortlisted for a Whitbread Prize.

One particularly intrepid bearer of the proud name of Pugh is the British environmentalist, marathon swimmer and maritime lawyer **Lewis Pugh**.

Born in Plymouth in 1969 and described as

"The Sir Edmund Hillary of swimming" – with reference to the British mountaineer of the name who scaled the heights of Mount Everest – he has endured several gruelling swimming ordeals to highlight the threat posed to oceans and rivers by global warming.

In 2006, he became the first person to attempt to swim the 26 mile (42 km) length of the River Thames to draw attention to the drought then afflicting England – thought to have been caused by climate change.

The swim took him 21 days to complete – having had to run part of the length because the drought had affected the river's flow – and he then lobbied Tony Blair for the UK to move towards a low carbon economy.

It was only a short time after this that the Prime Minister introduced the Climate Change Bill to Parliament, while Pugh was later granted the Freedom of the City of London.

One of his greatest feats came in 2007 when he undertook the first long-distance swim across the Geographic North Pole, and this was achieved by swimming across a 1km length of open sea.

He is also the first person to have completed a long distance swim in all five of the world's oceans – the Atlantic, Arctic, Southern, Indian and Pacific – to draw attention to the dangers posed to fragile ecosystems through global warming.

An inductee of the International Marathon Swimming Hall of Fame and a Fellow of the Royal Geographical Society, his many other honours and awards include South Africa's Order of Ikhamanga (Gold Class).

This is for his "exceptional sporting triumphs, humanitarian feats and creating consciousness about the negative effects of global warming."